TRADITIONS AND CELEB[RATIONS]

VETERANS DAY

by Charles C. Hofer

PEBBLE
a capstone imprint

Published by Pebble, an imprint of Capstone
1710 Roe Crest Drive
North Mankato, Minnesota 56003
capstonepub.com

Library of Congress Cataloging-in-Publication Data
Names: Hofer, Charles, author.
Title: Veterans Day / by Charles C. Hofer.
Description: North Mankato, Minnesota : Capstone Press, an imprint of Capstone, [2024] | Series: Traditions & celebrations | Includes bibliographical references and index. | Audience: Ages 5-8 | Audience: Grades 2-3
Summary: "Veterans Day is a holiday celebrated every November 11 in the United States. It honors military veterans who served in the U.S. Armed Forces. People often participate in a moment of silence to honor veterans and their service to the country. People also decorate with American flags and watch parades honoring the Armed Forces. Learn the ways people celebrate this special day and similar holidays in countries around the world"— Provided by publisher.
Identifiers: LCCN 2023001980 (print) | LCCN 2023001981 (ebook) | ISBN 9780756576059 (hardcover) | ISBN 9780756576004 (paperback) | ISBN 9780756576011 (pdf) | ISBN 9780756576035 (kindle edition) | ISBN 9780756576042 (epub)
Subjects: LCSH: Veterans Day—Juvenile literature.
Classification: LCC D671 .H58 2024 (print) | LCC D671 (ebook) | DDC 394.264—dc23/eng/20230113
LC record available at https://lccn.loc.gov/2023001980
LC ebook record available at https://lccn.loc.gov/2023001981

Editorial Credits
Editor: Aaron Sautter; Designer: Jaime Willems; Media Researcher: Rebekah Hubstenberger; Production Specialist: Whitney Schaefer

Photo Credits
Dreamstime: Joseph Morelli, 17; Getty Images: Brendon Thorne, 26, Brian Hendler, 27, Doug Mills-Pool, 23, FRANCE PRESSE VOIR/AFP, 25, Hulton Archive, 8, 9, 10, 13, Jose Luis Pelaez Inc, 29, Michael Loccisano, 19, MPI, 12, Spencer Platt, 5, 7, 18; Shutterstock: Jacob Lund, 15, Kamira, 20, Militarist, 14, Monkey Business Images, 1, Orhan Cam, 22, Steve Cukrov, cover

Design Elements
Shutterstock: Rafal Kulik

All internet sites appearing in back matter were available and accurate when this book was sent to press.

Printed and bound in China. PO5379

TABLE OF CONTENTS

Words in **bold** are in the glossary.

VETERANS DAY IS HERE

The streets are lined with red, white, and blue. A big band is playing. People wave American flags as a colorful parade marches down the street. It's Veterans Day!

Veterans Day is a special holiday in the United States. It's a time to celebrate the men and women who served in the U.S. armed forces.

Veterans Day takes place on November 11. It's a day to **honor** our nation's veterans. These are men and women who served in the **military**. They dedicated their lives to protect our country.

Veterans Day honors people who served in the past. It's a time to visit **memorials** and thank veterans for their service to our country. Veterans Day is an important part of our nation's history.

HISTORY OF VETERANS DAY

Veterans Day goes back to World War I (1914–1918). This war was fought by many countries in Europe. It was also known as the "Great War."

Ypres, Belgium, was mostly destroyed in World War I.

U.S. soldiers marching in France in World War I

The United States entered the war in 1917. By the end of the war, many cities in Europe were destroyed. Millions of people had died in battle. Many more were seriously **wounded**.

U.S. President Woodrow Wilson

On November 11, 1918, an **armistice** agreement ended major fighting in World War I. Later, a **peace treaty** was signed to officially end the war.

The next year, U.S. President Woodrow Wilson made November 11 a national holiday. It would be called Armistice Day. The holiday honored those who fought during the Great War.

Thousands of soldiers landed at Normandy, France, in World War II.

World War I was not the last war. The United States later fought in World War II (1939–1945). U.S. troops also fought in the Korean War (1950–1953).

In 1954, President Dwight D. Eisenhower changed Armistice Day to Veterans Day. The holiday would honor all those that served in the military. Today, Veterans Day honors those who served in times of war or in times of peace.

U.S. President Dwight D. Eisenhower

Veterans Day celebrates men and women who served in different **branches** of the military. These include the Army, Navy, Air Force, Marine Corps, and others.

Many veterans served overseas. These brave men and women spent time away from their families and friends. They worked hard to protect our country and keep us safe.

Veterans Day is different than Memorial Day. Veterans Day mainly honors veterans who are still alive. Memorial Day is a holiday that honors veterans who died while serving the country.

VETERANS DAY TODAY

There are many **traditions** on Veterans Day. One is a moment of silence. U.S. **citizens** pause for two minutes to honor veterans. It's a time to give thanks for their service.

Another tradition is to raise a U.S. flag. On Veterans Day, many homes and neighborhoods are decorated in red, white, and blue. Veterans Day is a time for Americans to show pride in their country.

Many cities and towns have big parades on Veterans Day. Veterans join in the parade. They walk in **uniform**. There are also floats and marching bands. Each celebrates a different branch of the military.

U.S. Marines marching band in a Veterans Day parade

A parade is a great way to honor our brave veterans. Join your friends and family. Go to a Veterans Day parade. Find some veterans and thank them for their service.

Vietnam Veterans Memorial
in Washington, D.C.

Some Veterans Day traditions are **somber**. It's a day to honor those who served. It's also a day to remember those who died while serving in the military.

On Veterans Day, some people visit memorials. These special places help people remember past wars. Many memorials honor those who died during a war. They also honor those who went missing.

The president of the United States takes part in a Veterans Day tradition. The president visits Arlington National **Cemetery**. This is a large cemetery in Washington, D.C. Today, about 400,000 veterans are buried at Arlington.

The president also visits the Tomb of the Unknown Soldier. This is a special memorial at Arlington. It honors those who have gone missing during times of war.

SIMILAR CELEBRATIONS AROUND THE WORLD

Other nations have holidays like Veterans Day. Canada and Great Britain celebrate Remembrance Day. It takes place on the second Sunday in November.

People in each country observe two minutes of silence. This time honors all the soldiers who served in their country's military.

Armistice Day ceremony in Paris, France

France and Belgium celebrate Armistice Day. These celebrations honor veterans and the end of World War I.

Australian soldiers march in an Anzac Day parade in Sydney, Australia

Australia and New Zealand celebrate Anzac Day. It takes place in April. This holiday honors soldiers from those countries who fought in World War I.

Israel celebrates Yom HaZikaron. It takes place in April or May. This holiday honors those who fought and died to defend the State of Israel.

The Armoured Corps' Memorial honors Israel's fallen soldiers near Jerusalem.

Veterans Day is a special day in the United States. It's important to honor those who served our country. It's also important to celebrate those who serve today.

Veterans Day is a proud day for all Americans. It's great to get involved in Veterans Day. Go to a parade. Visit a memorial. Be sure to thank veterans for their service!

GLOSSARY

armistice (AHR-muh-stis)—a temporary ending of fighting between two sides of a conflict

branch (BRANCH)—a section or part of a larger group

cemetery (SEM-uh-ter-ee)—a place where dead people are buried

citizen (SI-tuh-zuhn)—a member of a country or state who has the right to live there

honor (ON-ur)—to give praise or show respect to a person or thing

memorial (meh-MOHR-ee-uhl)—something that is built or done to remember a person or event from the past

military (MIL-uh-ter-ee)—the armed forces of a state or country

peace treaty (PEES TREE-tee)—an agreement between nations or groups to end a conflict

somber (SOM-buhr)—gloomy or sad

tradition (truh-DISH-uhn)—a custom, idea, or belief passed down through time

uniform (YOO-nih-form)—special clothes worn by members of a group

wounded (WOON-did)—injured or hurt

READ MORE

Ferguson, Melissa. *Celebrate Veterans Day.* North Mankato, MN: Pebble, 2019.

Jones, Emma. *Who Are Veterans?* New York: KidHaven Publishing, 2020.

Williams, S. *We Will Remember Them: The Story of Remembrance.* London: Franklin Watts, 2021.

INTERNET SITES

Arlington National Cemetery: The Tomb of the Unknown Soldier
arlingtoncemetery.mil/Explore/Tomb-of-the-Unknown-Soldier

Britannica Kids: Veterans Day
kids.britannica.com/kids/article/Veterans-Day/399637

Ducksters: Veterans Day
ducksters.com/holidays/veterans_day.php

INDEX

ABOUT THE AUTHOR

Charles C. Hofer enjoys writing books for young students. He's written many books about animals, culture, science, and sports for young readers to enjoy. Charles lives in Tucson, Arizona.